Verses of Faith & Freedom

21 Reflections on Life

Justin Terel Washington

Made with ❤ on the BookLeaf Publishing Platform
www.bookleafpub.in
www.bookleafpub.com

To my children—Malachi, Caleb, Laura, Adriel, Odeya, Jovonni, and my unborn son—You are my greatest poems, the living verses that breathe meaning into my life. Each of you carries a piece of my heart, and through you, I witness the beauty, strength, and promise of tomorrow. May these words serve as a reminder that you are loved beyond measure, that your stories hold immense value, and that faith will always be the bedrock beneath your feet.

And to my wife, Autumn—My rock, my refuge, my answered prayer. Through every storm and every victory, you have stood steadfastly beside me, never wavering, always believing. Your love is the rhythm that grounds me, the grace that uplifts me, and the reason I keep pushing forward. This book, like my life, is immeasurably richer because of you.

With all my love and gratitude,

Justin Washington

Acknowledgement

First and foremost, I give all honor and glory to Godâ€"my source, my foundation, and my greatest inspiration. Every word I write is a reflection of His grace, and without Him, none of this would be possible.

To my wife, Autumnâ€"my love, my strength, my greatest blessing. Through every trial and triumph, you have stood by my side, believing in me even when I struggled to believe in myself. Your love and support have been the rhythm that keeps me steady, and for that, I am eternally grateful.

To the poets and storytellers who have paved the wayâ€"thank you for reminding me that words hold power. Your creativity, passion, and courage to speak truth continue to inspire me to share my own.

And to you, the readerâ€"whether this is your first time reading my words or youâ€™ve walked this journey with me before, thank you. Thank you for your time, your attention, and for allowing these poems to find a place in your heart. I pray that within these pages, you discover something that speaks to you, moves you, and reminds you of the profound beauty of faith, love, and life itself.

With heartfelt gratitude,
Justin Washington

Preface

Poetry is more than mere words on a page—it's a reflection of the soul, a rhythm woven from faith, love, and the simple yet profound beauty of existence. This collection, *Verses of Faith & Freedom: 21 Reflections on Life*, takes you on a journey through the depths of emotion, the power of belief, and the wonder of human connection.

As a Black man rooted in faith, I have come to understand that life is a tapestry of trials and triumphs, moments that challenge us and those that remind us why we keep going. Each poem in this book is a testament to that journey. Some pieces whisper gratitude for life itself, while others wrestle with the mysteries of love, loss, and destiny. Through it all, one truth remains—God is ever-present, guiding each step, each verse, and each heartbeat.

These 21 poems are more than just words; they are prayers, praises, and reflections of the world as I experience it. They serve as a reminder that, no matter how vast the universe may be, faith grounds us, love elevates us, and our stories shape the heavens above us.

Thank you for allowing me to share this journey with you. May these words find you where you are and inspire you to embrace all that life has to offer.

—Justin Washington

Heaven's Alignment

They say—
The universe is always stretching.
And—expanding;
Far beyond what we can touch or see.
While we piece together mysteries
Of dark matter and gravity.
But none of that compares,
To how I'm entranced
By
YOU—
A quantum anomaly I can't undo.
The laws of physics,
They don't seem to apply,
When I'm near you.
Caught in your pull,
And orbiting your truth.
It's a rare twist of fate,
But here I am,
Held in your gravity
Lost in your design.
No force in space could tear us apart;
Your smile,
Outshines every star and every heart.

The constellations try,
But they can't align,
They couldn't form a pattern
To ever match your shine.
EVERY conversation,
With you,
Feels like a cosmic event.
Like—satellites transmitting
All your love—heaven-sent.
I know telescopes
Have seen incredible sights,
But none can compare to you.
Lighting up my nights.
You're a supernova,
That steals every scene.
An astral wonder that feels like a dream.
No black hole could ever,
Drag me away;
You're the gravitational force,
I'll always chase.
The cosmos bows to you,
And I don't mind the show—
Because you're the one,
I need more than they'll ever know.
I understand now,

Why Galileo never found your light.
If he had,
He'd have said,
The universe revolves around you,
EVERY NIGHT.

The Details

People say,
"The Devil is in the details,"
Well, I'm not a big fan of that.
I flip and say,
God is in the details—
Allow me to expand through facts.

Consider the stars, hand-stitched in the sky,
Or the sun's steady rise.
Every wave that crashes,
Each leaf that falls,
Echoes of a God who crafts,
Who sees, who calls.

I've heard some say it's by chance,
Or random math;
But even the hairs on our head are numbered;
He's mapped our path.
From Psalm to Romans,
He shows up time and again,
In every small crease,
He's the Author—THE END.

The lilies of the field?
Clothed in array,
He gave them colors to brighten our day.
If He decks out flowers and feeds every bird,
How much more will He cover us—His
Word?

People claim,
"Just coincidence!"
Or "Man, I was lucky!"
When blessings reign down.
But it's God's precision,
For He's always around.
Every door that opens,
Each door that's barred,
It's Him orchestrating,
With wisdom unmarred.

So next time you're tempted to doubt,
To sway,
Look closely—
His fingerprints mark the way.
In the details of life,
Big and small,
It's God,
NOT the devil,
WHO REIGNS OVER ALL!

From Shadows to Sunrise

I was born where Capitol dreams take flight,
In DC's glow—so bold and bright.
But fate unraveled, tearing love in two,
And sent me south with a heart bruised
through.

In Alabama's red dust, hope grew thin,
Where racism struck like a raging din.
Yet in that harsh and bitter land,
I found true friends, a steadfast band.

They stood by me through every dark night,
Their unity a beacon, a guiding light.
In whispered truths and silent cheer,
I learned that hope could conquer fear.

My mother's voice, both soft and wise,
Said, "Cream always rises to claim the skies.
Never look down—your feet on solid ground,
While God above, in endless love is found."

In youthful pride, I burned too strong,
A flame that blinded me for far too long.
On college fields where dreams were sown,
My scholarship was lost—a lesson painfully
known.

But then the Army called with steely might,
Teaching me to lock in, and fight the fight.
"Adjust, adapt, and overcome," they'd say,
Transforming my trials into strength each
day.

Now at thirty-nine, my scars are proof,
That every hardship bore a sacred truth.
From shadowed past to a rising sun,
I've learned that even broken hearts can be
won.

This is my story, raw and true—
A Black man's struggle, his hope renewed.
For in each detail, every trial's surprise,
I find God's fingerprint in every sunrise.

Kingdom Crossover: Faith's Final Stand

Step into my arena, devil—
The world is my battleground.
My combat boots stay laced,
The streets been callin' me Captain
America—
Now,
I ain't got a shield,
But I'm wielding His word.
I'm a sidekick to the Almighty—
His Robin in the field.
If you're playin' Joker,
I guess I'm the real Dark Knight.
I'll drag you through the shadows,
Straight into the light.
You're a clown with no purpose,
Just some parlor tricks and lies;
But I'm cuttin' through your BS,
Like Wonder Woman's lasso ties.

See,
My greatness was preordained.
Even when I take my shoes off,
I don't see defeat;
Because when I can't fight my battles,
God's fighting for me.
I mean,
I'm no Kryptonian,
But I gain my power from the Son.
Energized by the light,
Trust me devil—
You ain't built for this fight.

You're a punk in disguise,
I see you shapeshiftin',
Trying to throw me off—
It's giving Mystique-type vibes.
But I'm a Big Stepper,
Hulked up in my faith,
Smashing through your foul play.
I figured you out, my guy;
You're just another hater,
Tryin' to dim my sight.

Frontin' like you're Thanos with the stones,
But I'm armed with the Infinite—
His Word crushes your every thought,
Who needs to snap,
One whisper—
Striking down every demon you brought.

I'm strapped, devil,
I'm webbed up in truth;
Swingin' through the danger like Miles
Morales.
Faith stickin' to my soul,
Never missin' my shot,
Never losing control.
My spidey-sense tingling—
Don't try me, Sir.
I see you in the dark,
Pullin' strings,
But I'm on God's time.
I'm movin' with His power—
His mercy runs deep.
My Bible, like Thor's hammer,
It's seeking out all of my heathen—ways.
So please, step back, devil,
I'm suited in God's armor.

I don't need an arc reactor,
To power my faith.
Faith stronger than Vibranium,
Soul rooted in Zion.
You're no match for the power
That's surging through my veins—
Holy Ghost on fire,
Burning through your chains;
I guess I'm a Ghost Rider in flame.

I'm the Flash with the scriptures,
Speeding past your traps.
Your snares fall flat,
When I sprint through God's map.
Every dart you throw,
I deflect with His grace,
You thought you had me cornered,
But I'm always in His space.
So, bring your legions,
But I'm backed by heaven's host,
Archangels on my side,
Michael's leadin' the post.

I'm the Iron Man of faith,
My heart powered by His love,
Every time you strike me down,
I will ALWAYS rise above.
And when the final bell tolls,
You'll see who's truly won,
I'm standing in His victory,
A winter soldier of the Son.

Standing On Business

In the valleys of trials & tribulations,
I found solace—
Carved my own way.
And through shadows and doubt,
I learned how to pray.
And because the world threw me losses;
I've been scarred,
Bruised,
Beaten—
Broken.
Yet,
I stood firm—
Ten toes down in my darkest moments,
Although I was confused.

It took two Ls to C the truth so clear,
That in Christ, my purpose would persevere.
The letters of struggle,
The marks of pain,
Were just steps toward the heights where I'd
reign.

For I've always been standing on business,
You see,
Not just any business,
But His work in me.
An LLC, yes,
But so much more—
A life that's rooted in Christ,
Planted at my core.

Though the world may measure,
Success with gold,
I measure by the love that can't be sold.
In every loss—a lesson,
Every fall—a rise,
For standing on business,
Means trusting God's eyes.

So here I am,
With faith as my guide,
Standing on business,
With Jesus by my side.
Two Ls couldn't stop me,
They showed me the way,
To live for His kingdom,
In all I do, each day.

With garments of salvation wrapped around,
In His purpose,
I stand—firm on holy ground.
This venture's not mine,
But His work through me,
For in every stitch,
His love is what I see.

As I rise,
Let this business be a light,
A testament to the One,
Who reigns in might.
For I stand not in the shadows,
But in His grace,
Building His kingdom,
One step at a pace.

Prolific

Nipsey Hussle said,
"I'm prolific, so gifted,
I'm the type that's gonna go get it—
No kidding."
Prayers up to his family—sincerely,
Since his "Victory Lap" has finished.
The Marathon continues,
While most of us aren't even committed—
To the cause or the change.
We too focused on sex,
The money,
The fame.
We gotta switch up the mindset,
Time to change the frame—of thought.
J. Cole says it best,
"To the OGs, I'm thankin' you now,
Was watchin' you when you was pavin' the
ground,
I copied your cadence, I mirrored your style,
I studied the greats, I'm the greatest right
now."
Well I took heed.

See,
See I've been in my word—heavily...
Hebrews 11—Hereos of Faith...
Respectfully—I studied,
—I listened,
—I copied,
—I mimicked..
I got the glow now,
Bruce Leroy Faith,
I'm gifted.
Who's the baddest?
JE—SUS!!
That's why I don't follow the norm,
I'll be a weirdo for God.
Been a rebel since back in the day,
Don't run with masses,
Don't follow the wave.
I follow my Savior though,
He's lighting my way.
Through the valleys,
And shadows of death—
I am safe.
Ain't fearin' no evil,
Why?
'Cause I got His Grace.

My glow-up was real,
All sins got erased.
And,
I'm a better version of myself.
I took the advice of my predecessors,
I've diversified my wealth;
I secured the bag.
But more importantly,
I've sealed my fate—
Romans 1:16 faith.
See,
I have perfect peace.
Because in the end,
I know He loves me in-spite of my sin.
My Savior died,
But on the 3rd day,
He rose again,
So I could be free.
The blood that He shed,
He did it for all.
No matter your sin,
No matter the cause.
The God that I serve—
Well,
Well, He loves us ALL!

Therefore,
Prolific perception is what I desire,;
Prolific progression,
That's all I required.
My "Victory Lap" has not yet expired,
So I'm running with Jesus,
Until I retire.

Romans 1:16 (NIV)
16 For I am not ashamed of the gospel,
because it is the power of God that brings
salvation to everyone who believes: first to the
Jew, then to the Gentile.

aSilentPillar

When the world leans on me,
Seeking a steady hand—
I stand tall,
A fortress,
A rock in ever-shifting sands.
Their burdens weigh heavy,
And,
I know it's not my job, but—
I bear them with grace.
But who holds me,
When I need a safe space?

I am the pillar,
An unmovable force in the face of adversity.
The one they all trust,
In moments of doubt.
I am the friend,
Who answers the call.
But behind every strength,
There's a whisper of pain,
A heart quietly breaking under life's strain.

I've cried in the shower—
Too many times to count.
l break,
I even fold under the weight,
But I never back down,
Even when I KNOW I SHOULD.
But in the darkest hours,
When I stare the devil eye to eye.
When despair draws near;
I rise,
I stand,
And I walk boldly,
Embracing my fear.

When shadows grow long,
And my faith feels thin,
I turn to the One who dwells deep
within—GOD!
One of my favorite songs says,
"If you worship,
He will manifest Himself.
If you call Him,
He will manifest Himself
If you seek him,
He will manifest Himself."

Those words ring true
When my legs feel weak and begin to buckle.
In the stillness,
He comes,
Bringing peace and wealth.
In the chaos,
He's near,
Offering strength and health.
In the quiet,
He speaks,
Where my heart finds help.

He reminds me gently,
"You're never alone,
I'm your foundation,
You're unshakable—firm.
When you're the stronghold,
And no one's in sight,
Lean into My strength,
Let Me carry your night."

So, I trust in the process—
His timing—
His plans.

Knowing I'm cradled in the palm of His
hands.
Though I am the support,
The shoulder to cry on,
The one who has everyone else's back.
It's in Him I find refuge,
Where my soul can confide.
For I am never forsaken,
Never truly alone,
When I'm the one they turn to,
God keeps my back strong.
And in His embrace,
I find all I need,
A sanctuary of grace,
Where my spirit is freed.

And because I have God,
My knees will never buckle—completely.
And although I endure the suffering of my
peers,
I WILL NEVER FOLD!
I know it's not my battle,
But I have a giver's soul.
So I'm ten toes down,
With you through it all.

But just know,
Sometimes I still feel alone—
And I might need some space,
A silent pillar in need of embrace.
And that's when God reminds me,
"Son, do not fret—
I've got you.
Though the weight feels immense
And your heart feels pressed,
I am your rest,
Your peace.
When you are the pillar—
I AM YOUR CORNERSTONE!
And you my child,
You are never on your own."

So I rise up,
I stand tall,
Bearing the load of my loved ones;
Giving it my my all—
Because when I am weary,
I lean on God.

And in that strength,
I become a light,
Guiding my friends through their darkest
night.
For I know the way to ease their load,
It's found in surrender,
In letting go.
I show them the path,
To release their pain,
To call on God,
And let Him reign.

In the chaos,
In their fear,
I lead them to the One who's always near.
With open hands and a humbled heart,
I show them how to make a new start.
For just as I trust,
And just as I stand,
They too can find rest
In God's mighty hand.

So when they lean on me,
I guide them to see—
That the weight they carry
Isn't meant to be.
I point them to God,
To His love and His grace,
Where every burden can find its place.
For in surrender,
Their spirits will soar,
And the heaviness of life
Won't bind them anymore.
And with God by my side,
I'll be a beacon of support,
For the ones I love.
And in His embrace,
I find my purpose—
A silent pillar,
Locked in by faith.

G.O.A.T. Talk

See,
I was trained to kill—war hardened;
Heart was colder than Gretzky with the puck,
But God softened it.
I let my flesh die—Jesus,
So I could come alive.
I was reborn,
And now I thrive.
I'm Brady audibling at the line,
I peeped sin trying to blitz me.
With sin on my hipbone,
I hit 'em with my signature;
Fake the inside left and cut hard right—
Things got Messi.
Run up again Sir,
I'll show you what that Faith do.
I'll leave you wanting a career change,
Like a hit from Ray Lew—
Now I got 'em shook,
He can't tell his front from his back.
I'm in my bag now devil,
Ain't no stopping my attacks.

See,
I'm locked and loaded,
I keep some scriptures on me.
And I'll tee off like Tiger,
So you know that I ain't missing.
Now I'm starting to feel it;
Curving sin like Beckham,
And crossing him up like A.I.
I'm leaving sin defeated,
Like "Flu Game" Jordan—game 5.
But I can't lie,
Sometimes I'm exhausted.
And I lean against the ropes of life,
Willingly taking an onslaught of punches.
That's when I channel my inner Ali.
See,
I'm patiently waiting;
To find my lane,
And Bolt towards the finish.
But as I leave sin behind me,
I'm locked in on redemption,
Like Curry winning the MVP.
But me,
I'm built different,
I go back into the fray.

I prefer to remain in the trenches,
You know; where the demons stay.
I'm Sue Bird with the faith,
How I orchestrate my way—
Through trials and tribulations.
I DEMAND RESPECT!
And Satan,
You'll act—accordingly.
Because my legacy is etched in time—Kobe.
But don't tempt me,
I trained under my Father, and—
And we all know that ending.
Just call me Venus & Serena,
The way I'm living out my Father's lessons.
I've been great since a young age—
I'm high school Lebron crashing the lane,
Who gone stop me?
I'm Diana Taurasi on the isolation,
Who gone guard me?
NOBODY!
I'm pushing P on every block,
Purpose, praise, and progression.
I'm Michael Phelps with the passion,
The way I'm swimming in these blessings.

I'm Carl Lewis jumping over sin,
Shattering records.
I'm always on go mode,
Harvesting lessons.
Talk to me nice heathens,
Class is in session.
Simone Biles against the competition,
Defying inhibitions, second to none.
Guided by faith with every turn,
Victory is won.
And on my last day,
I transcended and my Father,
Told me,
"Well done!"

Ten Toes Testimony

First things first—
I AM HIM!
I've stood toe to toe with the devil,
And laughed in the face of sin!
Confidence at the highest level,
I don't ever see it diminishing.
God leads me,
But people say I'm tripping—
For not fearing the devil.
My response,
"Why fear what's not on my level"?
See,
I'll look him dead in his eyes,
And slap him—metaphorically, of course,
I'm nonviolent,
But let's be clear devil;
I smack harder than a meteorite,
And I tell my people not to stress.
Remain unphased,
By what haters on social media write.
I tell 'em to focus on your left side,
Cuz you got me to your right.

I evoke fear into sin,
Because God is leading my life.
Ten toes down,
Ten fingers uplifted;
As God is my witness,
I'm forever praising Jesus.
Sometimes I struggle though,
Don't get it twisted.
So many knives in my back,
I made a set with it.
They say iron sharpens iron;
So one by one,
I pull 'em out,
And sharpen my faith with it.
And I do that—faithfully.
And even still,
People hate on me.
And I won't lie,
It's devastating.
Have you ever had family & friends,
Questioning—
Why you love Jesus?
Why is church so important?
Why serve a God who allows so much
destruction?

My response,
"Why so concerned with my faith and how
my God functions?"
My trials and tribulations,
Brought peace and my purpose.
I'm chosen,
I walk this path boldly.
If Jesus can carry all of my burdens,
I can praise Him openly.
I said what I said,
Ten toes down,
Ten fingers uplifted;
As God is my witness,
I'm forever praising Jesus.

21 Reflections of Life

1. Life is a journey, a God-ordained test,
Each trial and triumph—His plan manifests.

2. Pain refines, like fire to gold,
But in His hands, you're never alone.

3. Love is holy, patient, and true,
A reflection of Christ in all that we pursue.

4. Fear will whisper, but faith will roar,
Step out of the boat—He's opened the door.

5. Money will fade, but His kingdom remains,
Seek first the Lord, not worldly gains.

6. Pride will crumble, bring man to his knees,
But grace lifts up, His mercy frees.

7. Forgiveness ain't weakness—it's Heaven's embrace,
For Christ forgave us, sin wiped with grace.

8. Your past is covered, redeemed by His
blood,
No chain can hold where His mercy stood.

9. Trust in His timing, His ways are best,
Every delay is a season of rest.

10. Family in Christ is deeper than blood,
Bound in His love, secure in His trust.

11. Words have power—speak life, not death,
Praise on your tongue, faith in each breath.

12. True success is a life well-spent,
Walking with God in love and intent.

13. Storms will come, but don't be afraid,
He's in the waves, His hand is your aid.

14. Every valley, every climb,
Is drawing you closer to His divine.

15. Joy is Jesus, no worldly thing,
His presence alone makes the heart sing.

16. Weakness is strength when placed in His hands,
Surrender is victory—watch where He stands.

17. The mirror shows flesh, but look past the frame,
See what He sees—you're called by His name.

18. Time is fleeting, eternity calls,
Live for the Kingdom, give Him your all.

19. God ain't silent, He speaks through the still,
Listen and trust—He's shaping your will.

20. Love without limits, forgive and extend,
Your light may lead the lost to Him.

21. Life is short, but Heaven is real,
Walk by faith—let His love be your seal.

HBCU Pride

In the beginning,
We learned in private.
Blacks were not good enough,
To learn where the whites did.
At times,
We studied in the same place God dwells—
The church.
Degrees which only "coloreds" could earn,
In classrooms where only Negros could learn.
And they did, with heads held high,
All while crosses were burned,
Right outside.
It's 2021 now,
Legacies etched in stone,
And filled with pride.
Private or public,
Community or university,
HBCUs promote growth and diversity.
Lawson State Community College,
Dillard and Xavier University.
Fisk, Alabama State,
Tuskegee and Tougaloo—
Spelman, the "House," and TSU.

All these were created,
Because The Institute for Colored Youth—
Founded in Pennsylvania, 1837.
184 years later,
We're 107 HBCUs strong.
Howard U,
Winston-Salem,
NC A&T.
St. Aug's, Grambling, and Benedict College,
Educating young minds,
With historical brown-skinned knowledge.
Schools like Alabama A&M,
Are creating a culture,
Where blacks can thrive.
Teaching the trades we need,
So we can strategically capitalize.
Florida A&M has the "Marching 100,"
They're a problem in the stands
Or on the field.
Alabama State's known for swarming
Hornets;
Their women's basketball team,
Is lights out with the jumpers.
Jackson State—"The Sonic Boom of the
South."

My mentor, my family, and I,
All walked these hallowed grounds.
Jackson Fair,
Jackson Dear,
THEE I LOVE,
HAIL TO THEE!
But I digress,
Southern U,
Reps the "Human Jukebox."
And their showmanship is second to none.
Their powerful sound,
And soulful arrangements,
Make any sporting event fun.
Prairie View A&M has the "Marching Storm."
They bring the thunder,
Amid the calm.
Wiley College,
Brought us "The Great Debaters,"
And old Savannah State,
Gives us the blue-orange Tigers.
A powerhouse of the South,
The band comes clawing.
We have Tuskegee University,
And it's famous Airmen.
They protected and served.

Represented a country,
That still shuns us to the world.
Regardless the school
Or their reputation,
Education is a priority,
The focus.
But that doesn't mean,
Sports,
Clubs,
The Band,
Aren't a primary motive—
To their success.
Scholar-Athletes,
They set the standard.
They are paving the way,
For future greatness.
Sorority rush, Fraternity row.
Some cross the burning sands,
While others say no.
We have Kappa Men,
Delta Divas and AKA's,
Iota Phi Theta,
The Men of Omega,
And their doggish ways.

Alpha Phi Alpha,
The refined man of the black & gold,
The Queens of Zeta Phi,
Sigma Men and Gamma Rhos.
Many will pledge,
While others won't.
Either route you choose,
We hear your voice.
Be free,
Be yourself,
Be black,
Achieve your goals.
Jackson Fair,
Jackson Dear,
The home I choose.
And where I roamed,
Thee, I love!
Hail to the college of my heart,
From JSU I will never part.
Hail to Thee,
Hail to Thee!
HBCU PRIDE!

Dopamine

The chemical messenger,
The "feel-good" chemical.
The body creates dopamine,
And it tells us to be happy.
Well,
The Lord calls me to be joyous,
So—God is Dope!
See,
God is the gravity,
That keeps me grounded.
It's why I stay in the light,
God handles my burdens,
Therefore my heart is lite.
A work in progress,
He's molding me right—
Into a masterpiece.
But I must remain malleable,
Approachable.
You can't be cool with God,
And continuously deny Jesus.
Out here okay with going to Hell right,
Rather than entering into Heaven, humble.

But I digress,
A talk for another day.
God is Dopamine!
He creates a joyous sensation;
My learning,
My memory,
My sleep,
My appetite,
My mood.
God is Dope!
This isn't your truth,
And that is fine.
I'd never force my beliefs,
But these are mine.
I won't argue my faith,
For you can rebuttal my words.
But my actions,
My joys,
They won't be unstirred.
Those are bound to my soul.

They're matching energies with God,
Like we're in Dragon Ball Z.
As I waltz the Fusion Dance,
I am free,
God Is So Dope!
And I have peace.

Eternal Rays

In the sky,
The sun rises bright and true,
Casting golden beams
As the morning's last dew—drops.
It warms the earth,
Giving life to all.
But beyond the skies,
A greater Light shines,
The Son of God,
In whom all hope aligns.
His love
Pierces the night,
Bringing warmth to hearts,
Igniting the inner light.
Just as solar panels gather
The sun's embrace,
So do we,
In His love—
We find our place.
Absorbing grace,
We are reborn.
Living reflections of His love,
Shining through.

In Him,
We find the power to grow.
Like flowers to the sun,
Our spirits glow.
He is our source,
Our eternal flame,
In the Son's light,
We are never the same.
So let us turn our faces
To His shining grace.
Basking in His love,
We find our space.
For as the sun fuels life
With its golden beam,
The Son fuels our souls,
Fulfilling every dream.
In solar energy,
A glimpse we see,
Of the boundless power
In Christ's decree.
For as the sun and Son
Give life and light,
In their warmth,
We find our true delight.

You've really been outta pocket lately—
Devil,
Don't make me,
Tuck you back in one!
Buried beneath,
The weight of His Word,
Crushed by the heel,
Of the risen Lord.
For every lie,
There's truth that breaks,
For every chain,
His love remakes.
You thought you won,
But check the score—
He rose. He reigns. Forevermore.

Turnipseed

Good day,
Gather round,
Behold what's in my hand,
And be amazed—
It's a turnip seed.
Small,
Brown,
And hidden—almost unseen.
It's nothing,
But a speck to the eye.
But oh,
MY GOD—
The Maker,
He designed it to defy!
The very limits of dirt and time,
To grow,
To reach,
To push,
Even climb.
You see,
My faith is like that tiny seed.

Dormant and dusty,
But filled with need—
Hunger and desire.
Like soil that's rich,
But needs the rain.
Faith seeks water,
Craves sun ("the Son"),
And endures pain.
"For if you have faith as small as this," He
said,
"You can move mountains; wake the dead."
Planted in darkness,
Buried in Earth,
It waits for light,
For warmth--
For birth.
And like our hearts,
When filled with His Word,
Our faith awakens,
Stirs,
And is stirred.
The roots dig deep,
The leaves reach high—
Faith, like a turnip,
Reaching the sky.

With strength that's hidden, silent, unseen,
It breaks through soil, pushes through green.
It's grit in the ground, it's grace in the dust,
It's a hard-won victory, it's a holy trust.
As it grows, it nourishes, provides,
Just like His Spirit moving inside.
This turnip, my faith, won't be swayed—
By winds, by storms, by unkind days.
It grows firm, like rock, strong as stone,
For it's tended by hands that call it His own.
Fed by the soil, by His love, it's fed,
By His promises spoken, His Scriptures read.
And one day, this seed once small,
Will be a harvest to feed them all—
A bounty of blessing, a feast divine,
Just like His love, like bread and wine.
For the Word is alive, like seed in the soil,
And the growth of faith? The fruit of our toil.
So hold that turnip seed,
Plant it deep.
In soil that's rich,
In soil that keeps ("firm foundation").
Water it with prayers,
Feed it with trust.

And watch it grow,
From dust to dust.
For what once was nothing,
So small and meek,
Now stands tall,
Strong,
And filled with,
The answer we seek.

Sin Whispers, Heaven Answers.

Let's take a walk,
Tell me your story,
And I'll listen to mine.
I'll pour out my soul,
So we can explore—dive deep.
Deep into the abyss of our minds,
Listen to my eyes,
See what I feel,
Hear what I see,
And touch what I understand.
Cross over that bridge,
and across those burning sands.
Come live my life,
Let me live yours.
Let's do forbidden things,
Leave our morals at the door.
Now, burn that bridge,
NEVER look back.
Why serve the Savior?
Why not serve yourself?
Why live in Heaven when you can live now?

I can give you everything just—
Just lie, cheat, and steal...
See time will reveal—
Money and power are everything.
So, by any means, you climb to the top,
Once on the throne and looking down,
Cut the rope—let 'em fall...
See, you did it on your own—solo dolo.
Take all the credit,
All the glory,
Anyone who doubts you,
Take them out.
Now the stage is set—
Your dark reign begins,
No chains, no conscience,
Just raw, ruthless wins.
Step boldly into the void,
Where angels fear to tread,
Let the whispers of damnation,
Fuel the fire in your head.
With every rule you shatter,
With every oath you break,
Remember: in this realm,
It's only power at stake.

Burn your past to ashes,
And embrace the night's call—
For sin is your kingdom,
And you will have it all.

But even as the night,
Seduces with its lies,
A Light persists—
Radiant, beyond disguise.
For God's love endures
Where shadows fall,
A beacon unyielding,
Outshining sin's call.
When the ashes settle,
And the echoes fade;
His grace rises strong
From what the dark once made.
No kingdom of deceit,
Can ever claim the throne—
In the Savior's truth,
We find our way home.
So cast aside,
The whispers of the fallen and weak.
For in His Light,
Redemption's voice will speak.

Though the devil tempts,
With a transient win,
God's eternal victory
Reigns deep within.

Sacred Alliance

My Rib,
On this day of renewed vows,
I stand before you
In a world,
Where shadows lurk,
And darkness schemes,
Yet here we rise—
Two hearts bound by faith,
United in a sacred dream.
You,
My dearest companion,
And eternal partner,
Are the beacon that guides,
My soul through every storm,
Steering our way with God's unfailing love.
Together we've journeyed down,
Winding roads of trials and flame.
Our marriage forged through prayer,
Our bond sealed in His holy name.
Every scripture has been our sword,
Every promise our shield,
In this life and beyond,
Our love stands strong—refusing to yield.

Across burning sands,
And crumbling walls of despair,
We've marched side by side,
With His Word forever there.
Your courage ignites a fire,
That no darkness can tame,
And in our united spirit,
Hope and love forever remain aflame.
Today,
I renew my vows to you,
My cherished friend and guide,
With a heart full of gratitude,
And eyes open wide.
For our union is a sacred alliance,
A testament to His decree,
A love that conquers every battle,
Setting our souls forever free.
In moments of strife,
And whispers of doubt that may arise,
Our marriage—
A fortress built on truth—
Reminds us to be wise.

The heavens resound with our steadfast,
Joyous cry,
As angels join our ranks,
Proclaiming love that shall never die.
So,
Let us stand together,
Against a world bent on strife,
For in our sacred alliance,
God breathes eternal life.
Though the enemy may tempt,
And darkness might enthrall,
In the radiance of His promise,
Evil is destined to fall.
As long as His Word,
Burns deep within our souls,
Our love will conquer every shadow,
Repairing broken parts to whole.
With faith as our guide,
And marriage as our sacred art,
We face the future boldly—
Two souls, one undivided heart.

On this anniversary,
I celebrate our journey—
Past, present, and what's to come,
For in you, my love,
I have found a home; with you, I am always
one.
Our sacred alliance,
Built on love and God's eternal decree,
Is the greatest victory of all—
A love that sets us free.

Light Up The World

Let there be light, He
spoke—and darkness fled in fear,
sunrise woke the world.

Genesis 1:3 (NIV)
3 And God said, "Let there be light," and
there was light. 4 God saw that the light was
good, and he separated the light from the
darkness. 5 God called the light "day," and the
darkness he called "night." And there was
evening, and there was morning—the first
day.

I Am My Father's Son

This is dedicated to my father, John Wesley
Washington, Jr., a beacon of inspiration
throughout my life—love you Pops!

I am my Father's son,
Forged in the fires of his essence
A blend of earth and heaven.
A rugged soul,
In the crucible of life,
I bear the Maker's touch.
A son of dust and divinity,
A paradox,
In whom I trust.
My Father,
The carpenter,
Shaped me with calloused hands.
His palms etched with splinters,
his heart a vast expanse.
He taught me to wield tools,
Not just of wood and steel,
But kindness,
Patience,
And the art of what's real.

He'd say,
"Son,
Life's grain runs rough,
Knots and twists.
But sand it down,
Polish the edges,
And love persists."
So I learned to mend fences,
Build bridges,
And repair.
To see beauty in imperfections,
To find purpose in the wear.
We'd cast our lines,
Into the river's ancient flow.
My Father's eyes crinkling,
Like the water's gentle woe.
He'd whisper,
"Patience, my boy,
For fish and life alike.
Sometimes the biggest catch,
Hides in the quietest strike."
And when storms brewed,
Waves crashing against our boat,
He'd steady the helm,
Unyielding, a steadfast devotee.

"Son," he'd say,
"Storms pass,
But anchors hold true,
Your faith, your roots—
They'll keep you steady too."
In a dim-lit bedroom,
We knelt side by side,
He embraced me in my weakness,
Providing comfort as I cried.
My Father's whispered prayers,
A river's silent tide.
He'd teach me to converse,
With the heavens above,
To wrestle with demons,
Seek solace,
And find love.
"Son," he'd murmur,
"God's ear leans close to your plea,
Pour out your heart,
Unfiltered, raw, and free."
So I'd spill my secrets,
My dreams, my doubts,
And in that sacred hush,
I'd glimpse eternity's route.

When shadows lengthened,
And the day wore thin,
My Father and I,
Would share a glass of amber sin.
He'd raise it high,
Eyes twinkling like distant stars,
"To life, to love,
To being more than what we are."
And we'd clink,
Savoring the burn,
The warmth,
Two men bound by blood,
By stories, by storms.
"Son," he'd say,
"Life's flavors blend bitter and sweet,
Sip slowly,
Taste every drop,
Let wisdom seep."
And when my Father rests,
Beneath the old oak trees,
His legacy woven into my bones—
My DNA.

I am my Father's son,
Both mortal and divine,
A flawed masterpiece,
A canvas molded from dirt,
To His grand design.
So I stand tall,
Shoulders squared,
Eyes toward the sun,
A man's man,
A child of God,
My journey has just begun.
For in the echo of his laughter,
And the echo of His love,
I AM MY FATHER'S SON—
Earthbound and heaven above.

Gloria Kennedy Studdard

Queen,
You were a beacon of light.
You cut no corners,
And for truth, you'd fight.
The lessons you passed on,
Will continue throughout generations.
Your legacy is etched in stone,
And from Heaven,
You're watching now.
Watching as your son,
Loves his family and saves lives.
Watching how your daughters,
Protect & serve and always rise—
To the occasion.
You changed countless lives,
Through love and compassion.
Your faith molded my faith,
Now, I walk with deeper understanding.
Nobody could prepare me for this pain,
This hurt buried deep within.

But—
I see your face and I smile.
I hear you fussing and I laugh.
You use to talk so fast;
Only the family understood you.
Grandy,
Thank you.
I know I told you while you were alive,
But I'll repeat it—thank you.
You shaped my mother's values,
And those were instilled in me.
You played a MAJOR role,
In the man the world now sees.
And Grandy—
Your great-granddaughter is here,
She's as precious as can be.
As your light dimmed,
Hers began to shine bright.
Now she is here,
And she has your eyes.
She has your smile,
And she has your grace.
She doesn't look like you though,
She has Autumn's face.

But we will instill everything you taught me;
Faith family honor achievement,
And give her all the love you brought me.
I love you,
And I miss you Queen,
My pain hasn't subsided.
But you once told,
"Don't ever let my pain win,
Our fates have been decided."
You smiled,
And I kissed your forehead,
And you said,
"Jus, take care of your mother,
Like she takes care of me."
I gave you my word Grandy,
I'll make sure you are proud of me.
I'll rise to every occasion,
I'll be the anchor for the family.
Let there be joy,
Let there be life.
A toast to the Queen,
The Studdard Matriarch!

Brotherhood Unshaken

X2

Bound by love, through thick and thin,
Rising together, we always win.
Through trials and tempests, Standing tall,
Hand in hand,
We never fall.
Holding each other, strong and true,
Every step, we push on through.
Rooted in faith, in trust, in light,
Heart's ablaze, hands gripped tight.
One bond unbroken, unshaken, real,
Our fellowship firm, our love the seal.
Day after day, through highs and lows.

Unity guides the path we choose.
Never alone, we lift, we fight,
Shining as brothers, beacons of light.
Hope in our laughter, strength in our tears,
Armor unyielding throughout the years.
Know that no matter how far we roam,
Each of us carries the love of home.
Never forgotten—one soul, one heart.

Through every trial, through every test,
My brothers stand; we give our best.
Bound by love, through thick and thin,
A fellowship strong, where all belong within.

Big brother John, the steady guide,
With wisdom deep and arms stretched wide.
A pillar firm, a voice so wise,
A lighthouse bright beneath the skies.

Antonio, fierce with fire inside,
A warrior's heart, a source of pride.
Bold and strong, he walks with might,
Never afraid to stand and fight.

Joshua's strength, steady and true,
Loyal and solid in all that we do.
A brother's keeper, firm in stand,
With an open heart and helping hand.

Brandon, the spark, the joy in the night,
Lifting us up, his soul shining bright.
A laugh, a word, a moment shared,
A brother's love beyond compared.

Tyrell, a man after God's own heart,
A servant leader, set apart.
With humble steps and hands that give,
He leads in love, he walks to live.

Aaron, a fighter who thrives and grows,
Defying the odds, his strength only shows.
No barrier holds him, no wall too high,
A testament true to faith that flies.

We gather close, no matter the call,
Through highs and lows, we rise, not fall.
Laughter and love, the anchor we keep,
Promises made, unbroken, deep.

No need for blood, no need for claim,
Brotherhood stands beyond just a name.
Through every season, through every call,
My brothers forever—I love you all!

The Testament of Justin

Once there was a little Black boy,
Born into a world both cruel and bright.
Where laughter echoed through city streets,
Yet shadows crept just out of sight.

He learned young that life ain't fair,
That hands ain't always meant to hold.
That love can cut, that words can tear,
And warmth can sometimes still feel cold.

Alabama winds howled truth too soon,
Taught him skin could summon disdain.
Taught him smiles don't always bloom,
And history still leaves a stain.

But he grew—oh, how he grew.
Carried burdens meant for men.
Fought through wars both seen and felt,
Never knowing where to begin.

Football dreams, pride too strong,
Cost him paths he longed to chase.
The Army taught him to march along,
To lock in, adjust, embrace.

Yet in the silence, pain still lurked,
Depression's whisper, razor-thin.
A night too dark, a step too close,
But God reached out and pulled him in.

See, God don't always shout His name,
Sometimes He just holds your hand.
Sometimes He lets the fire rage,
Then shows you how to stand.

Poetry became his saving grace,
Ink turned prayers, pain made art.
Every line, a scar unchained,
Every word, a healing start.

Now, he walks with peace inside,
A joyful man, no chains, no fear.
He battles demon with a grin,
Because he knows that God is near.

He laughs, he loves, he leads, he prays,
No longer lost, no need to hide.
And when they ask him how he made it,
He smiles and says,
"God never left my side."

www.ingramcontent.com/pod-product-compliance
Lightning Source LLC
La Vergne TN
LVHW051228200726
843510LV00011B/1509